SHORT WALKS
MADE EASY

YOR~~KSHIRE DAL~~ES

Ordnance Survey

Contents

Getting outside in the Yorkshire Dales		6
We smile more when we're outside		8
Respecting the countryside		11
Using this guide		12
Walk 1	Stainmore Railway and River Eden	**14**
Walk 2	Upper Swaledale Waterfalls	**20**
Photos	Scenes from the walks	26
Walk 3	River Swale at Reeth	**28**
Walk 4	Askrigg and Mill Gill	**34**
Photos	Wildlife interest	40
Walk 5	Dentdale	**42**
Walk 6	Ribblehead Viaduct	**48**
Walk 7	Upper Wharfedale at Buckden	**54**
Photos	Cafés and pubs	60
Walk 8	Horton in Ribblesdale	**62**
Walk 9	River Wharfe at Grassington	**68**
Walk 10	Malham Cove	**74**
Credits		80

Map symbols	Front cover flap
Accessibility and what to take	Back cover flap
Walk locations	Inside front cover
Your next adventure?	Inside back cover

2 Short Walks Made Easy

Walk 1

STAINMORE RAILWAY AND RIVER EDEN

Distance
3.1 miles / 5km

Time
1½ hours

Start/Finish
Stenkrith Bridge

Parking CA17 4SZ
Stenkrith Bridge car park, Nateby Road

Cafés/pubs
Kirkby Stephen

Lovely old railway path, River Eden meadows and woodland

Page 14

Walk 2

UPPER SWALEDALE WATERFALLS

Distance
2.4 miles/3.8 km

Time
1½ hours *CATCH A BUS*

Start/Finish
Keld

Parking DL11 6LJ
Park Lodge Campsite
car park (honesty box)

Cafés/pubs
Rukin's Teashop at campsite

Tumultuous waterfalls, serene Swaledale and peaceful garden

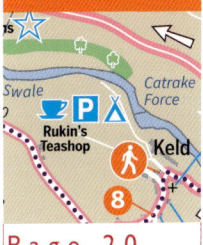

Page 20

Walk 3

RIVER SWALE AT REETH

Distance
2.9 miles/4.6 km

Time
1½ hours *CATCH A BUS*

Start/Finish
Reeth

Parking DL11 6TN
Reeth village green
(honesty box)

Cafés/pubs
Reeth; Grinton

Delightful River Swale and wobbly suspension bridge crossing

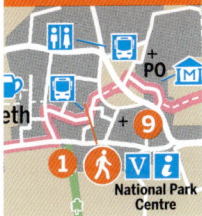

Page 28

Walk 4

ASKRIGG AND MILL GILL

Distance
2.3 miles/3.7 km

Time
1¼ hours *CATCH A BUS*

Start/Finish
Askrigg

Parking DL8 3HJ
Parkins Garth car park,
(honesty box)

Cafés/pubs
Askrigg

All Creatures Great and Small village, a cascade and grand views

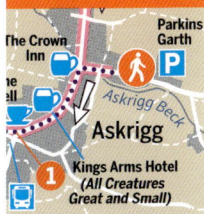

Page 34

Contents 3

Walk 5

DENTDALE

Distance
2.4 miles/3.9km

Time
1¼ hours *CATCH A BUS*

Start/Finish
Dent

Parking LA10 5QJ
Dent car park

Cafés/pubs
Dent

Hedgerows, hay meadows, flowers; intriguing Dales museum

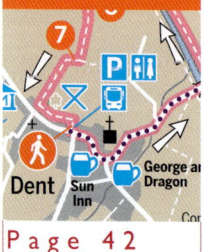

Page 42

Walk 6

RIBBLEHEAD VIADUCT

Distance
2.9 miles/4.7km

Time
1½ hours *GO BY TRAIN*

Start/Finish
Ribblehead Station

Parking LA6 3AS
Roadside parking beside B6255

Cafés/pubs
The Station Inn, Ribblehead

Magnificent viaduct; views to Whernside and Ingleborough

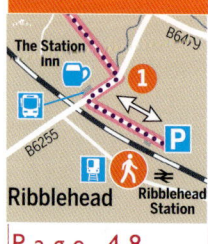

Page 48

Walk 7

UPPER WHARFEDALE AT BUCKDEN

Distance
3.9 miles/6.3km

Time
2½ hours *CATCH A BUS*

Start/Finish
Buckden

Parking BD23 5JA
National Park car park

Cafés/pubs
Buckden; Cray; Hubberholme

Exhilarating hilltop views and three cosy Dales pubs

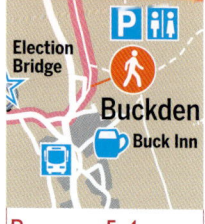

Page 54

4 Short Walks Made Easy

Walk 8

HORTON IN RIBBLESDALE

Distance
2.5 miles/4km

Time
1¼ hours *GO BY TRAIN*

Start/Finish
Horton in Ribblesdale

Parking BD24 0HG
National Park car park

Cafés/pubs
Horton in Ribblesdale

Riverside meadows and riparian walking on Ribble Way

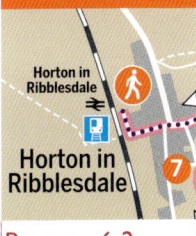

Page 62

Walk 9

RIVER WHARFE AT GRASSINGTON

Distance
2 miles/3.2km

Time
1 hour *CATCH A BUS*

Start/Finish
Grassington

Parking BD23 5AP
National Park car park

Cafés/pubs
Grassington

Lively Dales village, fly fishing, Linton Falls and riverside trail

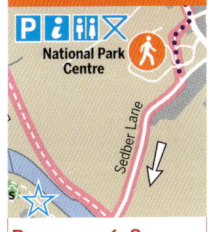

Page 68

Walk 10

MALHAM COVE

Distance
2.1 miles/3.4km

Time
1¼ hours *CATCH A BUS*

Start/Finish
Malham

Parking BD23 4DJ
National Park car park

Cafés/pubs
Malham village

Superb natural wonder of Malham Cove and re-emerging rivers

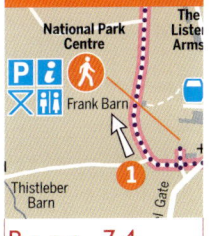

Page 74

Contents 5

GETTING OUTSIDE IN THE YORKSHIRE DALES

> " "
>
> In spring the traditional meadows are flower filled, aromatic and loud with birdsong

OS Champion
Debbie North

Pen-y-ghent seen across the River Ribble

A very warm welcome to the new Short Walks Made Easy guide to the Yorkshire Dales – what a fantastic selection of leisurely walks we have for you!

Established in 1954, the Yorkshire Dales National Park covers an area of 683 square miles across the three counties of Cumbria and North and West Yorkshire. There are more than 50 dales to explore in all, and walks featured in the book explore some of the better-known ones such as Swaledale, Wensleydale and Wharfedale, as well as less-frequented ones such as Dentdale.

The Dales is a farming landscape of pasture and hay meadows criss-crossed by a latticework of drystone walls and dotted with stone-built villages and field barns. In spring the traditional meadows are flower filled, aromatic and loud with birdsong. Yellow rattle, eyebright and red clover are just three of the many species of wildflower pictured in the 'Nature Notes' sections of these walks for you to look out for.

Walks take you to awesome natural wonders like Malham Cove and the tumultuous waterfalls at Kisdon Force; pass along tranquil, lush riversides at Grassington and Kirkby Stephen; take you under the engineering marvel that is the towering Ribblehead Viaduct; and lead to exhilarating, far-reaching views above Buckden, to TV film locations for *All Creatures Great and Small* and to cosy Dales pubs at Hubberholme and Askrigg.

Debbie North, OS Champion

WE SMILE MORE WHEN WE'RE OUTSIDE

Hay meadows beside Cray Gill

Whether it's a short walk during our lunch break or a full day's outdoor adventure, we know that a good dose of fresh air is just the tonic we all need.

At Ordnance Survey (OS), we're passionate about helping more people to get outside more often. It sits at the heart of everything we do, and through our products and services, we aim to help you lead an active outdoor lifestyle, so that you can live longer, stay younger and enjoy life more.

We firmly believe the outdoors is for everyone, and we want to help you find the very best Great Britain has to offer. We are blessed with an island that is beautiful and unique, with a rich and varied landscape. There are coastal paths to meander along, woodlands to explore, countryside to roam, and cities to uncover. Our trusted source of inspirational content is bursting with ideas for places to go, things to do and easy beginner's guides on how to get started.

It can be daunting when you're new to something, so we want to bring you the know-how from the people who live and breathe the outdoors. To help guide us, our team of awe-inspiring OS Champions share their favourite places to visit, hints and tips for outdoor adventures, as well as tried and tested accessible, family- and wheelchair-friendly routes. We hope that you will feel inspired to spend more time outside and reap the physical and mental health benefits that the outdoors has to offer. With our handy guides, paper and digital mapping, and exciting new apps, we can be with you every step of the way.

To find out more visit os.uk/getoutside

RESPECTING
THE COUNTRYSIDE

You can't beat getting outside in the British countryside, but it's vital that we leave no trace when we're enjoying the great outdoors.

Let's make sure that generations to come can enjoy the countryside just as we do.

Leave no trace

Keep dogs under control; bin and bag waste

Do not light fires; only BBQ at official sites

Leave gates as you find them

Keep to footpaths and open access land

Plan ahead for your trip

For more details please visit
www.gov.uk/countryside-code

USING THIS GUIDE

Easy-to-follow Yorkshire Dales walks for all

Before setting off

Check the walk information panel to plan your outing

- Consider using **Public transport** where flagged. If driving, note the satnav postcode for the car park under **Parking**
- The suggested **Time** is based on a gentle pace
- Note the availability of **Cafés**, tearooms and pubs, and **Toilets**

Terrain and hilliness

- **Terrain** indicates the nature of the route surface
- Any rises and falls are noted under **Hilliness**

Walking with your dog?

- This panel states where **Dogs** must be on a lead and how many stiles there are – in case you need to lift your dog
- Keep dogs on leads where there are livestock and between April and August in forest and on moorland where there are ground-nesting birds

A perfectly pocket-sized walking guide

- Handily sized for ease of use on each walk
- When not being read, it fits nicely into a pocket...
- ...so between points, put this book in the pocket of your coat, trousers or day sack and enjoy your stroll in glorious national park countryside – we've made it pocket-sized for a reason!

Flexibility of route presentation to suit all readers

- **Not comfortable map reading?** Then use the simple to-follow route profile and accompanying route description and pictures
- **Happy to map read?** New-look walk mapping makes it easier for you to focus on the route and the points of interest along the way
- **Read the insightful Did you know?, Local legend, Stories behind the walk** and **Nature notes** to help you make the most of your day out and to enjoy all that each walk has to offer

12 Short Walks Made Easy

OS information about the walk

- Many of the features and symbols shown are taken from Ordnance Survey's celebrated **Explorer** mapping, designed to help people across Great Britain enjoy leisure time spent outside

- National Grid reference for the start point
- Explorer sheet map covering the route

OS information
NY 772074
Explorer OL19

The easy-to-use walk map

- **Large-scale** mapping for ultra-clear route finding

- **Numbered points** at key turns along the route that tie in with the route instructions and respective points marked on the profile

- **Pictorial symbols** for intuitive map reading, see Map Symbols on the front cover flap

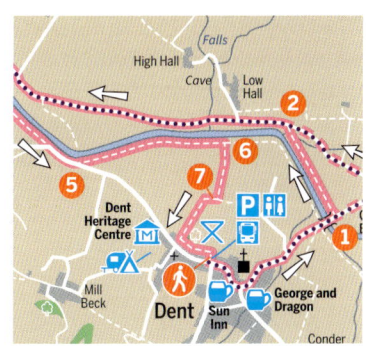

The simple-to-follow walk profile

- Progress easily along the route using the illustrative profile, it has **numbered points** for key turning points and **graduated distance** markers

- Easy-read **route directions** with turn-by-turn detail

- Reassuring **route photographs** for each numbered point

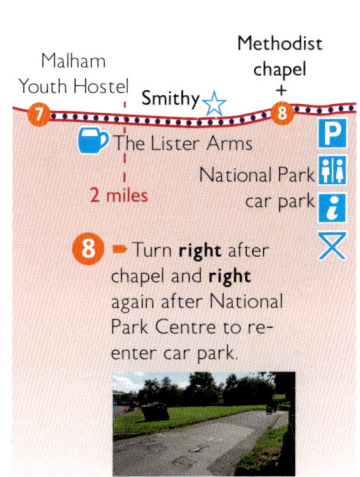

Yorkshire Dales 13

WALK 1

STAINMORE RAILWAY AND RIVER EDEN

The Upper Eden Valley and the Westmorland Dales lie on the north-western edge of the Yorkshire Dales, an enchanting area of gently rolling limestone grassland, farmland and scattered woods. This walk explores the area around the attractive market town of Kirkby Stephen, just outside the national park. After walking a stretch of the accessible Stainmore Railway, crossing two restored viaducts along the way, the route drops into the town. The final part follows the River Eden upstream, through meadows and woodland, and past some fascinating geological features.

OS information
NY 772074 Explorer OL19
Distance 3.1 miles/5km
Time 1½ hours
Start/Finish Stenkrith Bridge
Parking CA17 4SZ Northern Viaduct Trust's Stenkrith Bridge car park on B6259 (Nateby Road), 1 mile south of Kirkby Stephen town centre
Public toilets Kirkby Stephen, just before 5
Cafés/pubs Kirkby Stephen
Terrain Disused railway, quiet lanes, field paths (some surfaced), pavement and riverside trail
Hilliness Railway path flat, then gently undulating
Footwear Winter 🥾 Spring/Summer/Autumn 👟

14 Short Walks Made Easy

Public transport
Route starts 1 mile from Kirkby Stephen Railway Station

Accessibility
Wheelchair friendly on railway path and road sections; suitable for all-terrain pushchairs as far as ⑧

Dogs
Welcome but keep on leads. No stiles

Did you know? Visitors to Kirkby Stephen are often surprised to see macaws flying about the town. These scarlet, blue and yellow parrots were trained by the late John Strutt to return home for food and shelter after enjoying the freedom of the Upper Eden Valley's skies. A conservation charity he set up protects local habitats and also pays for the damage inflicted by these boisterous birds on people's roofs and chimneys.

Local legend Inside the church at Kirkby Stephen is the eighth-century Loki Stone, showing the figure of a bound devil, probably the shape-shifting Norse god Loki. Norse folklore, brought to this part of England by settlers from the north, shows him as a mischievous creature with unfathomable allegiances.

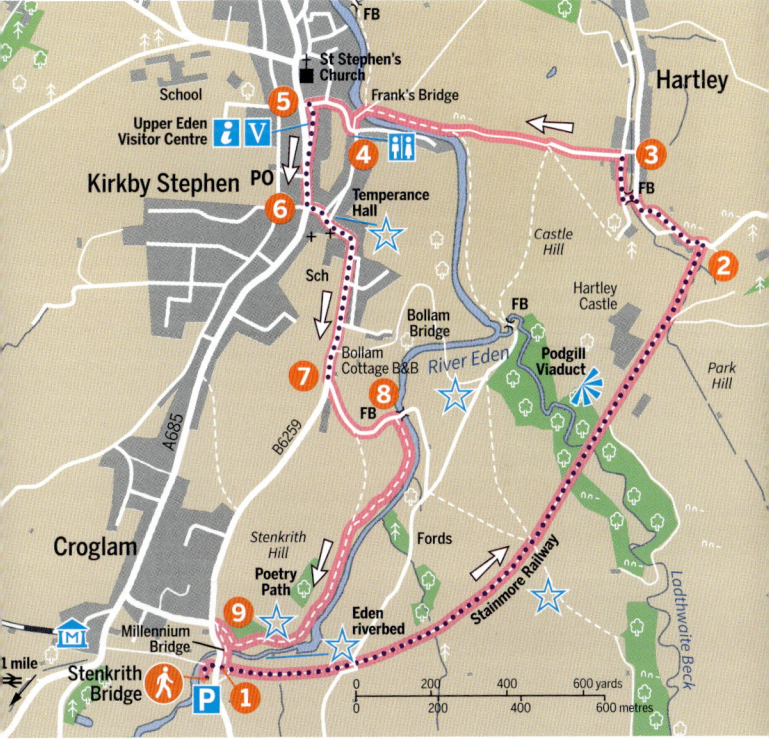

Walk 1 Stainmore Railway and River Eden 15

STORIES BEHIND THE WALK

☆ **The Stainmore Railway** In 1861, the Stainmore Railway opened between Barnard Castle and Tebay. It was originally constructed to carry coke from County Durham to blast furnaces in Cumberland and Barrow-in-Furness, and transport iron ore back to Cleveland. Most of the line was closed in 1962, although one section remained open until 1975. Two restored plate-layers' huts beside the disused trackbed contain information panels about the line's history and pictures of the railway when it was operational.

☆ **River Eden** The River Eden rises on the wild moorland above Mallerstang, a few miles south of Kirkby Stephen. It then meanders its way north along the base of the North Pennines through Appleby, Lazonby and Wetheral. Beyond the city of Carlisle, it spreads out over the immense marshes on the Scottish border, joining with other rivers as it ends its 75-mile journey to become the Solway Firth.

Stenkrith Bridge car park

Stainmore Railway — 1½ mile

- From car park's information panel, turn **left** along surfaced path heading downhill.
- Pass under road bridge to path junction.

1 ▶ Bear **right** at split, following old railway trackbed for 1 mile to lane. (After first viaduct, Podgill, watch for optional trail to 'viewing area' on left. Steps down to it accessed via kissing-gate to left of large farm gate.)

16 Short Walks Made Easy

☆ Poetry Path

Part of the walk follows the route of the Poetry Path which features 12 short poems elegantly carved into blocks of stone.
The verse, about hill farming and the local landscape, was written by the English poet Meg Peacocke, while the stone inscriptions were created by the letter-carving artist Pip Hall, whose studio is in Dentdale. Children are encouraged to take rubbings from the stones using paper and crayon.

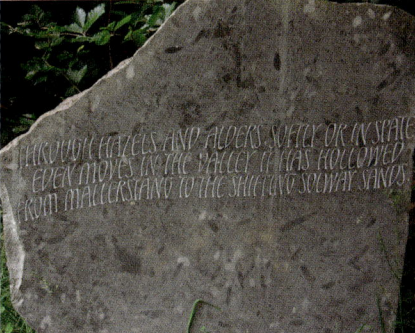

☆ Temperance Hall

The Temperance Hall, seen on the left just after ⑥, was built in 1856 on the site of the town's tannery yards. It would have been used to provide entertainment and talks for those who had taken the pledge to abstain from alcohol. The Temperance Movement, which sought to restrict the sale of alcohol, was at its peak in the second half of the 19th century and received support from religious groups including the Methodists.

Podgill Viaduct
1 mile
1½ miles

② ■ On reaching road turn **left**.
■ After 180 yards, and soon after right bend, go through gap in wooden railings on **left**. Path leads to lane.
■ Bear **right** along this for 90 yards to junction.

③ ■ Take track on **left** (beside house).
■ Later go through kissing-gate to descend field edge, eventually reaching River Eden.
■ **Cross** 17th-century stone bridge (Frank's Bridge).

Walk 1 Stainmore Railway and River Eden

NATURE NOTES

The sides of the railway path, as well as being lightly wooded with hawthorn, sycamore and birch, are home to oxeye daisy, dog rose and meadow cranesbill. Listen for the screech of buzzards circling overhead.

Down by the River Eden, you might see mallards near Frank's Bridge and grey wagtails. Beech, hazel, alder and sycamore can be found in the riverside woodland after ⑧, an area that is filled with the smell of wild garlic in the spring. This is a particularly interesting section of the river, as the water has carved unusual shapes into the bedrock, a mixture of limestone and sandstone fragments known as brockram. From the Millennium Bridge after ⑨, look down on the churning waters as they make their way through massive, cauldron-like bowls.

Keep your eyes peeled for red squirrels. Although not found in much of England, these native creatures continue to survive in this area.

Wild garlic

④ ▶ A few strides beyond bridge, turn sharp **right**, climbing steps between buildings.
▶ At top, go **right** again. Follow lane round left bend.

⑤ ▶ Just before church entrance portico on right, turn **left**.
▶ After passing in front of shops and to left of Upper Eden Visitor Centre, **join** pavement along main road for 150 yards to fork.

⑥ ▶ Bear **left** here – along B6259.
▶ Pavement ends after 500 yards along this road – just before Bollam Cottage B&B.

18   Short Walks Made Easy

Brockram

Meadow cranesbill

Red squirrel

River Eden ☆ Poetry Path ☆ Eden riverbed, interesting geology ☆ Stenkrith Bridge car park

8  2½ miles **9** 🅿 3 miles

7 ▪ Take footpath on **left** immediately after B&B – signposted Stenkrith and Nateby.
▪ Path ends at River Eden.

8 ▪ Go through gate on **right**.
▪ Walk with river on left – grass at first, later entering woodland.
▪ Having followed river for ½ mile, path swings up to **right**. (Ignore trail on left.)

9 ▪ Reaching T-junction near gate, turn **left**. Cross Millennium Bridge (footbridge) over River Eden.
▪ Path splits on far side. Bear **right** and pass under road bridge to retrace steps to car park.

Walk 1 Stainmore Railway and River Eden 19

WALK 2

UPPER SWALEDALE WATERFALLS

OS information
NY 892012 Explorer OL30
Distance 2.4 miles/3.8km
Time 1½ hours
Start/Finish Keld
Parking DL11 6LJ Park Lodge Campsite car park (with honesty box)
Public toilets Keld
Cafés/pubs Rukin's Teashop at campsite
Terrain Mostly stony paths and tracks; some road walking; rough path to Kisdon Upper Force recommended only for sure-footed
Hilliness Steadily undulating; steep path to Kisdon Upper Force

If you want to see waterfalls, the Yorkshire Dales is the place to come. And, within the Dales, the Upper Swaledale area around Keld has some of the best. This walk visits East Gill Force and the two falls that make up Kisdon Force. The spur path to the latter is rough and might not suit everyone, but even if you choose to miss it out, you'll still enjoy a beautiful walk accompanied all the while by the sight and sound of the magnificent River Swale.

20 Short Walks Made Easy

Footwear
Winter
Spring/Summer/
Autumn

 Public transport
DalesBus services 30 (Mon-Sat) and 831 (Sun and bank holidays): dalesbus.org

Accessibility
Wheelchair friendly on road sections and as far as ❶; suitable for all-terrain pushchairs, apart from Kisdon Force trail

Dogs
Welcome but keep on leads. No stiles

Did you know? Brothers Richard and Cherry Kearton, born in the neighbouring hamlet of Thwaite in 1862 and 1871 respectively, were two of the world's first wildlife photographers. Cherry went on to become a film-maker and shot the earliest footage of London from the air in 1908.

Local legend At least two of the buildings between Keld and Muker, two miles away, have spooky reputations. There's said to be a haunted barn that was inhabited by 'fiendish imps' who terrorised the local people. They even chased a school master to his death. Another story tells of how a farmer's daughter came to a horrific end after setting fire to her clothes. Her night-time cries filled the farmhouse long after death and, when her family could stand it no longer, they ended up fleeing.

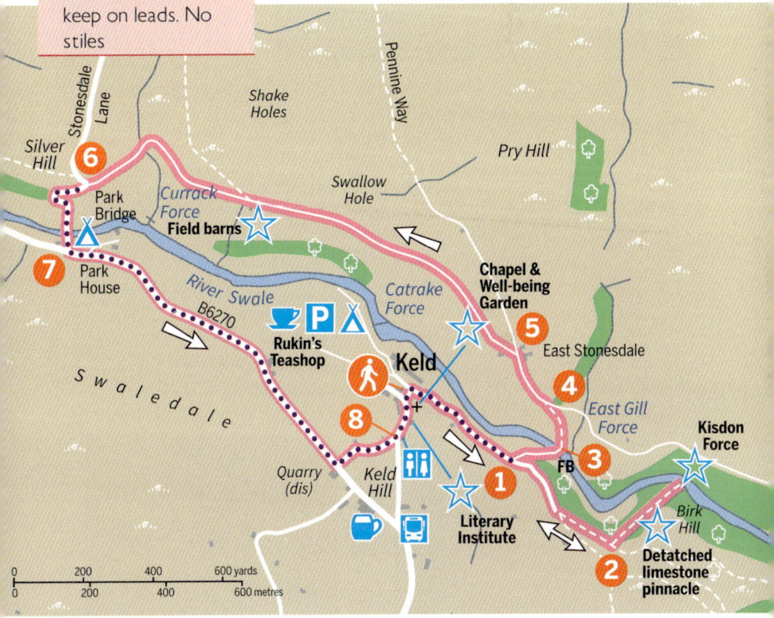

Walk 2 Upper Swaledale Waterfalls

STORIES BEHIND THE WALK

☆ **Field Barns** Stone laithes, or field barns, are a familiar feature of the meadows of the Yorkshire Dales. In Swaledale, they're often referred to as cow 'uses (cow houses). Hay was stored on the upper level of the buildings, ready for feeding the cattle that used the ground floor. In recent years, the Yorkshire Dales National Park has been working with owners to restore many of these barns and, in some cases, find new uses for them.

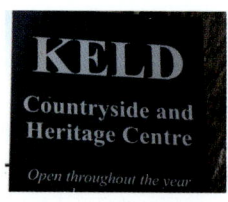

☆ **Literary Institute** The restored stables of the old Literary Institute have been home, for the last few years, to the Keld Countryside and Heritage Centre. Open to the public, it contains lots of fascinating information about the people and traditions of the dale. Next door, the restored school building contains more displays and artefacts.

Park Lodge Campsite car park
Rukin's Teashop

Detached limestone pinnacle ☆   Kisdon Force

½ mile

🟥 Leaving car park via vehicle entrance, keep **straight ahead** and take gravel path to right of small building – signposted Swale Trail. Reach path split in 250 yards.

① 🟥 Bear **right** at fork, although you'll return to take left-hand option after visiting waterfall.
🟥 About 140 yards after gate, watch for fingerpost on right.

22 Short Walks Made Easy

☆ **Waterfalls** There are several waterfalls along the River Swale near Keld. The two falls that make up Kisdon Force are possibly the most dramatic, as the river plummets through a narrow, wooded limestone gorge. East Gill Force, which can also be seen on this walk, forms a pretty 'curtain' across the rock just above the footbridge. Catrake Force, near Park Lodge Campsite, is made up of a series of four small waterfalls, while further upstream Wain Wath Force forms pools popular with summer bathers.

☆ **Chapel and Well-being Garden** Keld's independent chapel came into being in 1789 after the minister, Edward Stillman, raised the £700 needed to build it by walking from Keld to London, seeking donations along the way. Up until then, he had been preaching in barns and people's homes. The well-being garden was created next to the churchyard in 2010 as a place for people to sit and relax amid wildflowers and fruit trees.

❷ ▶ Fingerpost points to Kisdon Upper Force. Branch **left** to it along trail – rough and slippery later.
▶ After viewing falls, return to ❶ and turn **right**, downhill.

❸ ▶ Immediately after footbridge, bear **left** to ascend stony path to fingerposted junction. (Easy 50-yard detour on grass to right provides view of East Gill Force.)

Walk 2 Upper Swaledale Waterfalls

NATURE NOTES

One of northern England's most iconic sheep breeds originates from this beautiful valley. The Swaledale, characterised by its black face, white nose and curly horns, is the emblem of the Yorkshire Dales National Park.

In spring and early summer, listen for the call of waders including oystercatcher, lapwing and curlew. Great spotted woodpeckers can often be heard hammering on trees.

The meadows encountered after ❺ contain a huge range of wildflowers including bird's-foot trefoil and harebell. Other species include lady's bedstraw, meadow buttercup, thistles, red clover, common rock-rose and cow vetch.

If you choose to take the path down to Kisdon Force, watch for the tall limestone pinnacle that has become detached from the main crag up to the right.

Limestone pinnacle

☆ Field barns

☆ River Swale

1½ miles

❹ ► Go **left** at T-junction – along rough track, soon climbing steeply. After 160 yards, track goes through gate and gradient eases towards next junction.

❺ ► Bear **left** as track forks. Follow this for ⅔ mile to lane

❻ ► Turn **left** at road. There's a sharp bend, but traffic tends to be light. **Cross** River Swale to reach T-junction with B6270.

Short Walks Made Easy

Swaledale sheep

Harebell

Curlew

Bird's-foot trefoil

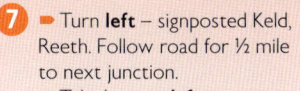

2 miles

Literary Institute ☆
Chapel and Well-being Garden ☆
Park Lodge Campsite car park 🅿
Rukin's Teashop ☕

7 ➡ Turn **left** – signposted Keld, Reeth. Follow road for ½ mile to next junction.
➡ Take lane on **left** – signposted Keld only.

8 ➡ Go **left** at T-junction in hamlet, opposite public toilets.
➡ At bottom of lane, turn **left** again to re-enter car park.

Walk 2 Upper Swaledale Waterfalls 25

This page (clockwise): Upper Swaledale;
Pen-y-gent, one of the Yorkshire Three Peaks;
East Gill Force; Ribble Way at Horton in
Ribblesdale
Opposite (clockwise): Ribblehead Viaduct; Swing
Bridge over River Swale; Winterscales Beck

WALK 3

RIVER SWALE AT REETH

After rushing down from the hills, the River Swale begins to broaden and slow down as it passes below Reeth. Starting from the Richmondshire village that once played a key role in the Industrial Revolution, this walk explores a delightful part of Swaledale. Passing through meadows along the way, it drops into the valley bottom to join riverside paths. After crossing the wobbly suspension bridge, it pays a visit to Grinton before returning to Reeth, where pubs and cafés greet hungry and thirsty walkers.

OS information

SE 037992
Explorer OL30

Distance
2.9 miles/4.6 km

Time
1½ hours

Start/Finish
National Park Centre, Hudson House, Reeth

Parking DL11 6TN
Reeth village green (honesty box)

Public toilets
Opposite The Buck (top end of Reeth village green)

Cafés/pubs
Reeth; Grinton

Terrain
Tracks and lanes through village; meadows; riverside paths (short section on boardwalk)

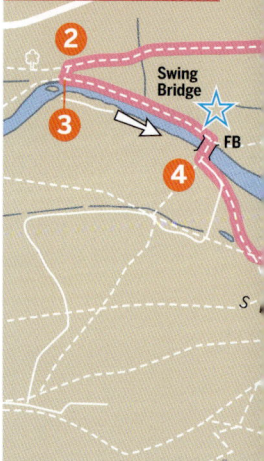

28 Short Walks Made Easy

Did you know? The Coast to Coast long-distance walk passes through Reeth. Alfred Wainwright devised the 190-mile route in 1972, having been inspired by the opening of the Pennine Way, the country's first National Trail, in 1965. Starting in St Bees in Cumbria and ending in Robin Hood's Bay in North Yorkshire, the Coast to Coast crosses three national parks – the Lake District, the Yorkshire Dales and the North York Moors.

Local legend On the moorland above the River Swale at Grinton is a large, square rock named on Ordnance Survey maps as John Moss's Chair. Nobody knows who John Moss was, although it has been suggested that he may have been one of the many giants of Dales folklore, or possibly a local spirit.

Hilliness
Mostly flat but with one short, steep descent and one short, steep climb

Footwear
Winter
Spring/Summer/Autumn

Public transport
DalesBus services 30 (Mon-Sat) and 830/831 (Sun and bank holidays): dalesbus.org

Accessibility
Suitable for pushchairs as far as ②

Dogs Welcome but keep on leads. No step stiles but five squeeze stiles with gates

Walk 3 River Swale at Reeth

STORIES BEHIND THE WALK

☆ **River Swale** The infant River Swale is fed by becks that have their sources on the Pennine moorland that straddles North Yorkshire's border with Cumbria. The river meanders downstream past Keld, Muker, Gunnerside and Reeth before leaving the Dales near the market town of Richmond. It flows on past Catterick and enters the River Ure near Boroughbridge, its waters finally reaching the North Sea at the Humber estuary.

✝ **St Andrew's Church, Grinton**
St Andrew's at Grinton was built in the 12th century, possibly on the site of an earlier Saxon chapel. For several centuries it served the largest parish in Yorkshire. With no other consecrated ground in the area, corpses used to be carried from as far afield as Keld, 13 miles away, for burial at St Andrew's. This ceased in 1580 when a new church was built in Muker.

National Park Centre   ½ mile

- With your back to National Park Centre, turn **right** into Anvil Square. After following lane round to right, keep **left** along pathway to left of wall. This joins lane from right.
- Go **left** at T-junction.

1 - At next T-junction, turn **right** – signposted Doctor's Surgery.
- When lane ends, go through gate and keep **straight on** across fields for 600 yards.

30 Short Walks Made Easy

☆ **Swing Bridge** The first pedestrian 'swing' bridge over the River Swale near Reeth was built in 1920. This was damaged beyond repair by floods on 19 September, 2000. The river is said to have risen almost 10 feet in 20 minutes during heavy rain, causing an uprooted tree to hit the bridge destroying cables and abutments. The structure that stands here today, almost identical to the original, was built in 2002.

Lead mining

The hills above Reeth are littered with the spoil heaps, shafts and buildings associated with the lead mining industry. The area's minerals have been exploited since at least Roman times, but it was during the Industrial Revolution that the lead mines of northern England became the busiest in the world. This important metal was being plundered from the hills to roof, plumb and paint the homes of Britain's rapidly expanding towns and cities.

 Swing Bridge | 1 mile River Swale

2 ▶ After three narrow meadows in a row, each accessed via gated squeeze stiles, enter larger field and walk **downhill** with wall/fence on left.
▶ Trail enters wooded area and descends **right**.

3 ▶ Go through gate at bottom and immediately **left** through second gate.
▶ Follow riverside path for 350 yards, sometimes on boardwalk.
▶ **Cross** Swing Bridge over River Swale.

Walk 3 River Swale at Reeth 31

NATURE NOTES

In spring and summer, the road and track verges are brought to colourful life by a range of wildflowers. Watch for red campion, meadow cranesbill and common mallow, among others. Common mallow has edible parts including its leaves and seed pods. It can also be used as a poultice for wounds. Common blue and gatekeeper butterflies might be seen in the meadows and along verges.

The route also passes through grassy meadows and along lightly wooded sections of the valley bottom, including the riverbank itself. Among the species found are sycamore, ash, hazel, hawthorn, holly, elder, blackthorn and bramble. Sycamores live for up to 400 years and their female flowers develop into 'helicopter' fruits called samaras. Elder, blackthorn and bramble produce edible berries — respectively known as elderberry, sloe and blackberry.

Sloes on a blackthorn bush

4 ▶ Having crossed, turn **left** and walk beside fence on right.
▶ After small footbridge, take gravel path **left**. Follow it for ½ mile to lane.
▶ Go **left** along road for 350 yards.

5 ▶ A few yards short of 30mph limit sign, go through squeeze stile in wall on **left**. Descend steps and swing **right**.
▶ Keep **straight on** along rough lane beside St Andrew's Church to village road.

6 ▶ Turn **left** at T-junction. Walk along road for 140 yards.
▶ Immediately after road bridge, go through gated gap in wall on **left** and follow fenced path between fields to re-meet road.

32 Short Walks Made Easy

Above: sycamore samaras
Below: elderflowers

Top: common mallow
Above: common blue

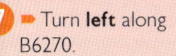

2½ miles

7 ▶ Turn **left** along B6270.
▶ After road bridge, and just before Reeth sign, go **left** as if to follow track but then immediately turn **left** again to access Beck Side Path.
▶ Stroll 120 yards to gate.

8 ▶ Pass through small gate on **left** and follow fenced path, soon climbing. Emerge onto cobbled lane.

9 ▶ Turn **right**. Follow lane round to left.
▶ With Post Office on right, **cross** village green to return to Hudson House on far side.

Walk 3 River Swale at Reeth 33

WALK 4

ASKRIGG AND MILL GILL

The attractive village of Askrigg, used as a key location in the filming of the original *All Creatures Great and Small* TV series, lies in the middle reaches of Wensleydale. This walk passes through the centre of the village on its way to Mill Gill, once used to provide power for local businesses. The route goes through wildflower meadows and sumptuous woodland, and pays a visit to an impressive waterfall before returning along an old walled track with great views of the surrounding countryside.

OS information
SD 950911
Explorer OL30

Distance
2.3 miles / 3.7 km

Time
1¼ hours

Start/Finish
Askrigg

Parking DL8 3HJ
Parkins Garth car park (honesty box), Leyburn Road

Public toilets
None

Cafés/pubs
Askrigg

Terrain
Village walkways, roads, flagstones, woodland trail, grassy meadows and stony tracks

Hilliness
Undulating

Footwear
Winter
Spring/Summer/Autumn

34 Short Walks Made Easy

Public transport
DalesBus service 156 Mon-Sat, dalesbus.org; the Little White Bus operates on Sundays and can be booked by calling 01969 667400

Accessibility
Wheelchair friendly as far as ②; pushchairs also from ⑧ until end

Dogs
Welcome but keep on leads. No stiles, but four small, awkward gates with steps

Did you know? Wensleydale is probably best known for its cheese. This crumbly, creamy cheese is said to have evolved from a recipe brought from France by Cistercian monks in the 12th century. At that time, it was made from ewe's milk; today it is made from cow's milk. Large-scale commercial production of the cheese began in 1897 in Hawes, a few miles from Askrigg, at a creamery that's still in business today.

Local legend According to local legend, Wensleydale was once home to a giant, a descendant of Thor. Like many giants, he was a rather mean fellow and was feared by local people. Eventually though, he was killed by his former faithful hound and only friend, Wolfhead, whom he had betrayed.

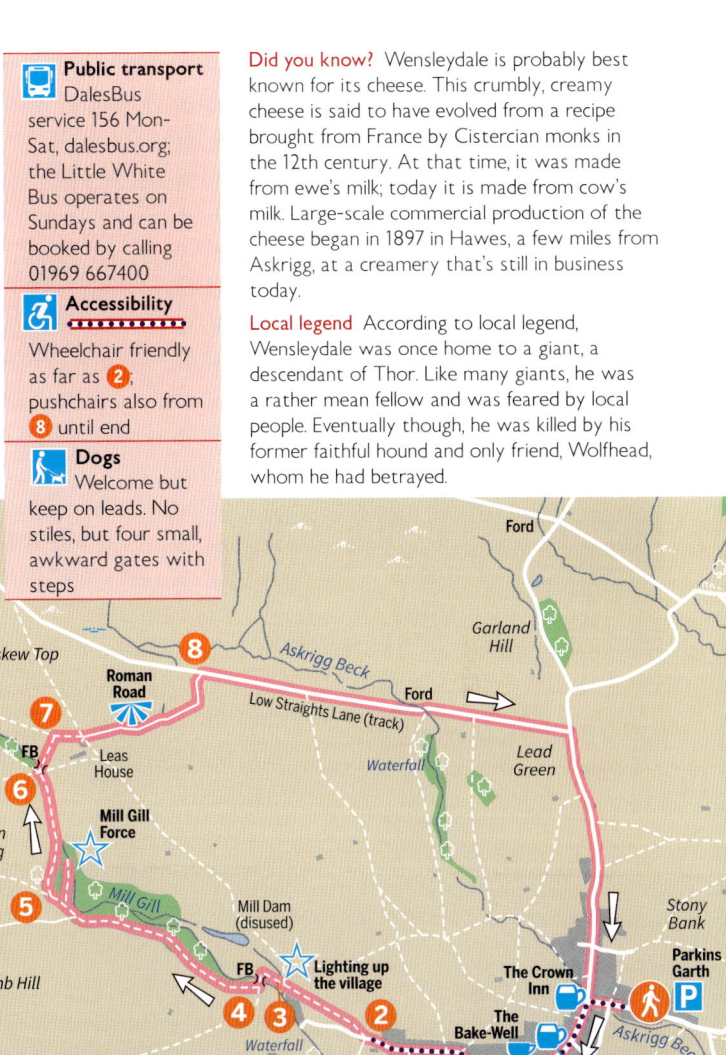

Walk 4 Askrigg and Mill Gill 35

STORIES BEHIND THE WALK

🫖 All Creatures Great and Small

Askrigg, with its fine old houses, was used as a location for the filming of the original *All Creatures Great and Small* TV series, which began in 1978 and ran right through the 1980s. It became the fictional Darrowby where the veterinary practice of James Herriot (played by Christopher Timothy) was based. The village's Kings Arms Hotel became the fictional Drovers Arms. A new version of the series, filmed partly in Grassington (see Walk 9), first aired in 2020.

☆ Lighting up the village

Electricity came to Askrigg relatively early – in 1908 – thanks to the owner of Mill Gill House, William Handley Burton, who had been using the beck to power his sawmill for several years, installed a dam above the nearby waterfall and piped water into a building housing a turbine. The electricity generated was used for lighting villagers' homes.

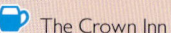

Kings Arms Hotel ① 🫖 *All Creatures Great and Small* ② **Lighting up the village** ☆ ③

½ mile

The Bake-Well ☕
🅿 Parkins Garth car park
🫖 The Crown Inn

- Leave car park and turn **right** along Leyburn Road.
- Follow road round to left – signposted Hawes – to walk into village centre.

① ▶ Just after The Bake-Well café, turn **right** along lane beside church. This becomes rough track leading to gates.

② ▶ Go through gate to **right** of Mill Gill House's gateway. (Sign asks to keep in single file.)
- On far side of meadow, go through gate and pass to right of old building.

36 Short Walks Made Easy

☆ **Mill Gill Force** The waterfall on Mill Gill lies in an impressive, steep-sided gorge just below the main path through this gorgeous, wooded valley. Sketched by the painter JMW Turner and described by the poet William Wordsworth as "delightful and delicious", it spills over a lip of rock to enter a tremendous amphitheatre that can only be seen from the lower path. Be careful if you venture into the bottom of the gorge because the damp rocks here are very slippery.

Roman Road

As you climb the rough track leading up to ⑧, take a moment to look over your right shoulder for a view of the long ridge to the south-west. You might just be able to make out an old lane climbing the side of it. This is the Cam High Road; it follows the line of a Roman road that led south-west from the fort at nearby Bainbridge (Virosidum) to Burrow in Lonsdale.

Mill Gill Force ☆

1 mile

③ ▶ Turn **right** at fingerpost immediately after building.
▶ Walk through woods with beck on left at first, then cross footbridge.
▶ Turn **right** after gate at top of steps.

④ ▶ Quickly re-enter woods via gate. Follow path for 500 yards to fork.
▶ Main route goes **left** – still in woods – to path junction in 50 yards.
▶ (Right-hand fork leads, in 80 yards, to base of Mill Gill waterfall – well worth a visit.)

Walk 4 Askrigg and Mill Gill   37

NATURE NOTES

The meadow after ❷ is full of wildflowers in summer including speedwell, meadow buttercup, red clover and yellow rattle, but it's the plethora of oxeye daisies, looking like a cover of unseasonal snow from a distance, that inevitably draws the eye.

In spring, Mill Gill's woodland floor is home to a succession of wildflowers. Primroses are among the first to appear, followed by the white flowers of wild garlic and then bluebells. The tree species found here include sycamore, some rather grand old beech trees and rowan, which sports red berries in the autumn.

On the higher ground beyond ❼, there's a good chance of seeing lapwing. Swallows frequent this area in summer too, while wrens can be seen all year round. One of Britain's smallest birds, the wren is surprisingly loud, its charming song often ending with a distinctive trill.

Rowan berries

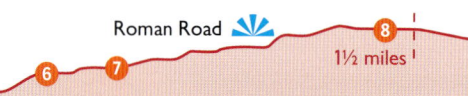

❺
- Keep **right** at fingerpost.
- Leave trees at next gate, keeping close to wall on right.
- Pass through two meadows and, 200 yards after leaving woods, go through small gate in wall on **right**.

❻
- **Cross** gated footbridge hidden in trees directly below fingerpost.
- On far side, follow narrow trail **half-left** up grassy slope ahead to wall corner.

38 Short Walks Made Easy

Bluebells

Above: oxeye daisies
Below: swallow

Low Straits Lane (track) | 2 miles

Parkins Garth car park 🅿

7 ▸ At corner, turn **right** – signposted Low Strait – crossing pathless ground for 50 yards to reach farm gate.
▸ Go through gate and join rough track climbing away from farmhouse up to track junction.

8 ▸ At T-junction, turn **right** along walled track for ½ mile to reach lane.
▸ Turn **right** along it. Descend steeply into Askrigg.
▸ Go **left** at T-junction to retrace steps along Leyburn Road. (Car park on left in 90 yards.)

Walk 4 Askrigg and Mill Gill 39

Opposite (clockwise):
Swaledale sheep; wren
This page (clockwise):
peregrine falcon; red campion;
hay meadow; Well-being
Garden, Keld; thistle

WALK 5

DENTDALE

Lying on the western edge of the Yorkshire Dales National Park, idyllic Dentdale is carved into a patchwork of stone-walled enclosures. Old barns, farmhouses and picturesque cottages are scattered across its lower slopes, while the River Dee snakes along the valley bottom beside traditional hay meadows and patches of woodland. This easy walk through a gentle landscape starts from the tranquil village of Dent and uses riverside lanes and meadow paths to explore the dale.

OS information
SD 704870 Explorer OL2
Distance 2.4 miles/3.9km
Time 1¼ hours
Start/Finish Dent
Parking LA10 5QJ Pay-and-display car park in Dent
Public toilets In car park
Cafés/pubs Dent
Terrain Roads (including cobbled section) and meadow paths
Hilliness Mostly flat apart from short descent on road to river and slight slope leading back into car park at end
Footwear Winter 🥾 Spring/Summer/Autumn 👟

42 Short Walks Made Easy

| **Public transport**
S3 Western Dales Community Bus operates three services a day, Mon-Fri; Dent railway station is more than 4 miles from village |
|---|
| **Accessibility**
Wheelchair and pushchair friendly as far as ③ (using alternative route between ① and ②) |
| **Dogs**
Welcome but keep on leads. Two step stiles (one with dog gate); two gated squeeze stiles with steps |

Did you know? Dent was the birthplace, in 1785, of the British geologist Adam Sedgwick. He was one of the founders of modern geology, identifying both the Cambrian and Devonian periods. Charles Darwin was one of his students, but, as an Anglican priest, Sedgwick was firmly opposed to Darwin's theory of evolution.

Local legend The Sill family, who derived their wealth from Jamaican plantations worked by slaves, lived in Dentdale in the 18th century. That much is known. It's also a fact that they brought slaves to England to work in their Dentdale home. What remains a mystery is the location of the burial ground in the valley where these slaves' remains were interred. Or, more intriguingly, whether there's any truth in the story that Emily Brontë based Heathcliff, in her novel *Wuthering Heights*, on one of the Sills' slaves.

Walk 5 Dentdale 43

STORIES BEHIND THE WALK

☆ **The three counties** When you reach the road junction at ③, look to the left and, beyond the meadows, you'll see the high ground rising to Crag Hill. Just beyond this, but out of sight at this point, are Gragareth, the highest point in Lancashire, and Whernside, Yorkshire's highest hill. Dent itself used to lie within the West Riding of Yorkshire, but has fallen within the boundaries of the ceremonial county of Cumbria since the 1974 local government reorganisation.

☆ **Dales Way**

The meadow paths beside the River Dee follow the route of the Dales Way. This 80-mile walking route from Ilkley in West Yorkshire to Bowness-on-Windermere in Cumbria passes through two national parks – the Yorkshire Dales and the Lake District. It largely follows riverside trails and other valley routes, making it a relatively straightforward introduction to long-distance walking.

Sun Inn
George and Dragon

Church Bridge, River Dee

Wheelchair/pushchair users to follow alternative route on map

½ mile

- From car park entrance, turn **left** along road, soon walking on cobbles.
- When road splits in front of George and Dragon pub, bear **left** and walk to river.

① ▶ Immediately after crossing River Dee, go through tiny gate in bridge wall on **left** and cross field. (Those with limited mobility can continue for 200 yards and take lane on **left**, rejoining the walk at ②.)

44 Short Walks Made Easy

⭐ Hay meadows

Since the mid-20th century, hay meadows like these have become increasingly rare. The timing of mowing is crucial for their continued existence and for the many species of wildflowers, insects and birds which thrive in them. Most farmers prefer silage over hay as a winter feed for livestock because its production is less weather dependent. However, the cutting of silage represents one of the greatest threats to traditional meadow plants, because it is cut too early and too frequently for them to set seed.

🏛 Dent Heritage Centre
The village museum, the Dent Heritage Centre, houses an eclectic collection of artefacts relating to life in the valley over the last few centuries. Moving mannequins and stuffed animals jostle for space with old toilets and a working model of the Settle-Carlisle railway. Panels on the walls tell the story of the 'terrible knitters' of Dent, renowned for their speed and unusual method of knitting.

1 mile

② ➡ Meadow trail leads to stile. Cross this and turn **left** along lane. (Limited mobility users rejoin main route here.)

➡ Ignoring two tracks on right, continue on lane for more than ¾ mile to Barth Bridge.

③ ➡ At T-junction, turn **left** along road.

➡ Immediately after crossing Barth Bridge, go through gated gap in wall on left and descend steps to follow trail across meadow.

Walk 5 Dentdale 45

NATURE NOTES

It is an absolute joy to walk through the meadows of Dentdale just before the hay is cut in the summer. They are full of wildflowers, including yellow rattle and eyebright. Both these plants are used by farmers when recreating traditional meadows – their roots fix to grass roots, weakening the grasses and allowing other species to become established.

The verges and hedgerows of the lane between ❷ and ❸ are also a riot of colour in summer, home to dog rose, hawthorn, meadow cranesbill, cow vetch, oxeye daisy, yellow loosestrife and the highly invasive ground elder.

Above: yellow rattle and eyebright
Left: red clover

Barth Bridge, River Dee ❸ — The three counties ☆ — ☆ Hay meadows ❹ — 1½ miles — ☆ Dales Way

❹ ▪ After footbridge and gate leading into third meadow, grassy trail swings **half-right** to rejoin river.
▪ **Continue** on riverbank path along edge of hay meadows for 500 yards to road.
▪ Turn **left** at road.

❺ ▪ Walk along road for 90 yards, take narrow trail through vegetation on **left**, leading to gate beside river.
▪ Route continues along edge of another two meadows to stile.

46 Short Walks Made Easy

Common toad, distinguishable by its dry, warty appearance, while the skin of a frog is smooth and slimy

Speedwell

Dog rose

Dent Heritage Centre (150 yards)

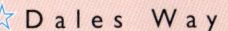

2 miles

☆ Dales Way

6 ▶ On entering third meadow via stile, turn sharp **right**, walking with wall on right.
▶ After next gate, continue along right-hand edge of meadow. In far corner, go through small gate on **right**.

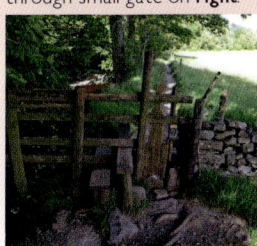

7 ▶ Walk with another wall on left for 25 yards and then turn **left** through kissing-gate.
▶ About 30 yards along this trail, turn **left** through gap in wall. Head across picnic area on **right** to re-enter car park.

Walk 5 Dentdale 47

WALK 6

RIBBLEHEAD
VIADUCT

Ribblehead Viaduct is one of the most remarkable pieces of railway engineering in Great Britain. Its 24 arches span a distance of 440 yards, towering more than 100 feet above the surrounding moorland. Starting from Ribblehead Station on the Settle-Carlisle Railway, this walk heads out across the moorland and passes under the massive viaduct. Then, using a combination of farm lanes and tracks in the shadow of Whernside, Yorkshire's highest hill, it comes back round to view the amazing structure from another angle.

OS information
SD 765789 Explorer OL2
Distance 2.9 miles/4.7km
Time 1½ hours
Start/Finish Ribblehead Station
Parking LA6 3AS Station car park for rail users only; roadside parking beside B6255, near its junction with B6479
Public toilets Station toilets for rail users
Cafés/pubs The Station Inn, Ribblehead
Terrain Mostly good tracks and surfaced lanes; short sections of rougher track
Hilliness Short ascent on rough track leading up to ⑥; descent on steps just before ⑦
Footwear Year round

48   Short Walks Made Easy

Public transport
Settle-Carlisle railway stops at Ribblehead: settle-carlisle.co.uk
DalesBus services 830, 831 (seasonal) to the Station Inn: dalesbus.org

Accessibility
Wheelchair and pushchair friendly as far as ⑤

Dogs
Welcome but keep on leads. No stiles

Did you know? Winterscales Beck is typical of streams and rivers in limestone country, appearing and disappearing on several occasions. They flow happily over impermeable rock and then vanish on reaching permeable limestone, the water seeping down through bedding planes and joints. The river progresses underground until another layer of impermeable rock is reached and the water then re-emerges on the surface.

Local legend Watch for the Weather Forecasting Stone on the front wall of the Station Inn at Ribblehead. Although the inn was first licensed in 1879, the stone is a more recent addition. It has become part of Three Peaks' folklore, poking gentle fun at the British obsession with the weather and bringing a smile to the face of walkers seeking shelter and refreshment.

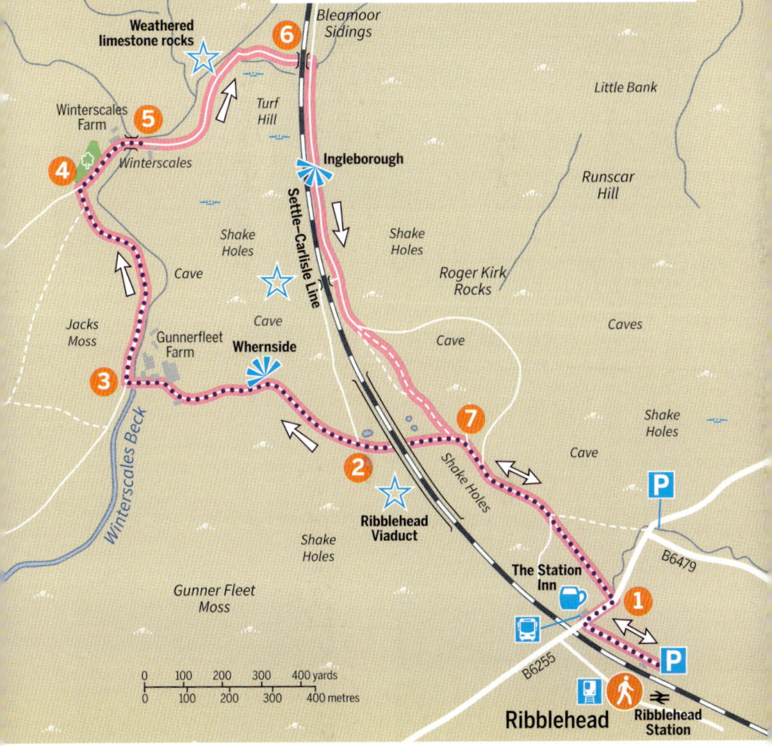

Walk 6 Ribblehead Viaduct 49

STORIES BEHIND THE WALK

☆ **Settle–Carlisle Line** This was the last English railway built almost entirely by hand. Work on it began in 1869 and, at the height of construction, about 6,000 workers were involved. They came from all over Britain and Ireland, often bringing their families with them and living in overcrowded, unhygienic hut settlements on the boggy moors. Many died as a result of industrial accidents and diseases such as smallpox.

Whernside At 2,415 feet above sea level, Whernside towers over much of this walk. Although it is the highest hill in Yorkshire, its trig pillar actually lies just within the boundaries of neighbouring Cumbria. Before the local government reorganisation of 1974, Yorkshire's highest peak was the 2,585-foot Mickle Fell, which lies further north in the Pennines. This is now the highest point in County Durham.

- From station platforms, walk into car park and **down** access lane towards B6255.
- Turn **right** along main road for 80 yards to pedestrian gate beside cattle grid.

① ▶ Just beyond cattle grid, take broad path on **left**.
- Narrower path soon joins from right. Then, as another path goes right, keep to broader path as it swings **left** to pass under viaduct.

50 Short Walks Made Easy

☆ **Ribblehead Station** The historic station at Ribblehead is one of ten maintained by the Friends of the Settle–Carlisle Line, a charity set up in 1981 when the line was threatened with closure. Volunteers from the group look after the gardens and carry out minor repairs. The station is also home to a small visitor centre with displays about the history of the railway and a virtual tour featuring aerial photography.

Ingleborough
Along with Whernside and Pen-y-ghent, Ingleborough (2,371 feet) makes up the trio of hills known as the Yorkshire Three Peaks. Its distinctive outline, including its flat top and tiered north-east face, is visible at several points on this walk. The hill covers a massive area, much of which is maintained as a National Nature Reserve that is home to limestone-loving plants and animals.

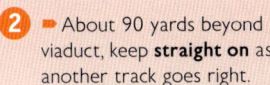

Whernside · Gunnerfleet Farm ❸ ❹
1 mile

❷ ➡ About 90 yards beyond viaduct, keep **straight on** as another track goes right.
➡ Keeping to left of farm sheds, go through pedestrian gate beside cattle grid and continue to junction.

❸ ➡ Turn **right** along lane, with Winterscales Beck on your right at first.
➡ Walk to next lane junction.

Walk 6 Ribblehead Viaduct 51

NATURE NOTES

Climbing to almost 1,100 feet above sea level, this walk visits some of the highest ground encountered in this book. The wildlife reflects this with moorland grasses and sedges covering large areas. In spring and summer, the wetter ground is covered in the distinctive white tufts of cotton grass, also known as bog cotton. It has been used in the production of paper and candle wicks, but is too brittle for textiles. Cuckoo flower, also known as lady's smock, can be seen in similar areas, its pale pink flowers heralding, like the cuckoo, the arrival of spring.

The pink,tubular flowers of foxglove can be seen growing beside the railway. Although the plant is generally poisonous, it contains the chemical digitalis, used to treat high blood pressure and heart problems.

Top: cuckoo flower
Above: blue-faced Leicester sheep

Winterscales Farm — 1½ miles — Weathered limestone rocks ☆ — ⑥ Settle–Carlisle Line — 2 miles — Ingleborough

④ ▪ At T-junction turn **right** – signposted Whernside.
▪ As one track branches left up to farmhouse, keep **right**, quickly crossing humpback bridge – signposted Whernside – to next set of buildings.

⑤ ▪ Here, keep **left**, rising along rougher track to gate.
▪ Immediately after gate, keep **left** as less obvious track goes right.
▪ **Continue** for 500 yards to railway.

52   Short Walks Made Easy

Foxglove

Top: cotton grass
Above: limestone outcrops beside Winterscales Beck

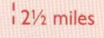
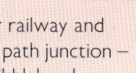
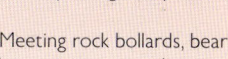

2½ miles

(Roadside parking 200 yards)

The Station Inn

Ribblehead Station

6 ➤ Pass under railway and turn **right** at path junction – signposted Ribblehead.
➤ Soon after gate, **descend** stone steps.
➤ Walk with railway on right to junction in front of viaduct.

7 ➤ Meeting rock bollards, bear **left** to rejoin outward route.
➤ Retrace steps: keep **right** as one path goes left and then turn **right** at road. Station's access lane is opposite pub.

Walk 6 Ribblehead Viaduct 53

WALK 7

UPPER WHARFEDALE AT BUCKDEN

This walk climbs a little more than others in this book, but the rewards are well worth the extra effort. Ascending the old track up Buckden Rake allows walkers to gaze down on beautiful meadows that bring colour and life to Upper Wharfedale in spring and summer. Bees and butterflies fly among the wildflowers, while waders call from the hillsides and hares dash across the paths. Down in the valley bottom, the countryside is sprinkled with Dales favourites – field barns, waterfalls and cosy country pubs.

OS information
SD 942773
Explorer OL30

Distance
3.9 miles/6.3km

Time
2½ hours

Start/Finish
Buckden

Parking BD23 5JA
National Park's Buckden pay-and-display car park

Public toilets
In car park

Cafés/pubs
The Buck Inn, Buckden; The White Lion Inn, Cray; The George Inn, Hubberholme

Terrain
Stony tracks, grassy meadows, country lanes and surfaced riverside path. When wet, exposed limestone on paths is slippery

54 Short Walks Made Easy

Hilliness
Undulating, including long ascent at start; flat after halfway mark

Footwear
Winter 🥾
Spring/Summer/Autumn 🥾

🚌 **Public transport**
DalesBus services 72A/72B and 874/875: dalesbus.org

♿ **Accessibility**

Wheelchair and pushchair friendly only on road sections

🐕 **Dogs**
Welcome but keep on leads. Two gated squeeze stiles

Did you know? Buckden is on the route of a Roman road that linked forts at Ilkley (Olicana) with Bainbridge (Virosidum) in nearby Wensleydale. The Romans were in this area to exploit minerals found in the hills, particularly lead.

Local legend In 1964, a skeleton of a man was found in the disused lead mine above Buckden. Known as Buckden Bill, he was wearing studded leather boots, trousers, shirt, waistcoat and felt hat. He was said to be in a relaxed pose, with his hands folded across his chest. The contents of his pockets, including a clay pipe and coins, suggested he'd died in the early 1890s. But why? The mine had already been closed for several years, and he was found in a tunnel that was difficult to access. We'll probably never know.

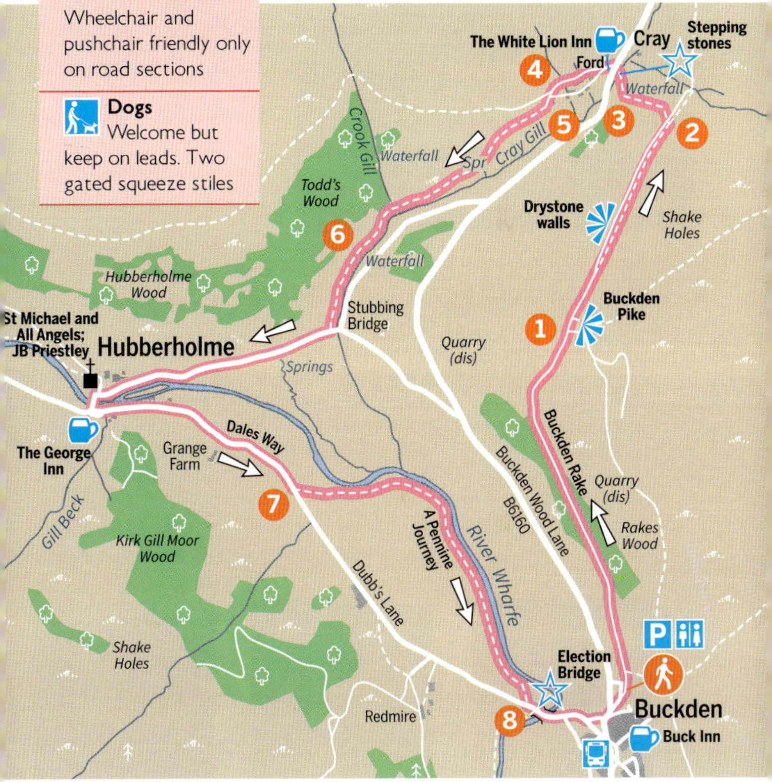

Walk 7 Upper Wharfedale at Buckden 55

STORIES BEHIND THE WALK

🔆 **Buckden Pike** In its early stages, the walk crosses the western slopes of Buckden Pike. At 2,303 feet above sea level, this is one of the highest points in the Yorkshire Dales. The southern end of its summit plateau is home to a memorial to five Polish airmen who died when their plane crashed here in 1942. The sixth member of the crew survived by following fox prints through the snow to the village of Cray.

🔆 **Drystone walls**
As in much of the Dales, drystone walls line the sides of Upper Wharfedale and divide the valley bottom into small meadows. Some date from medieval times, although long, straight walls typical of the higher ground are more closely associated with the enclosure acts of the 18th and 19th centuries. The walls are built without mortar; stability being achieved through traditional construction methods.

Buckden Rake

Buckden Pike 🔆

Drystone walls 🔆

½ mile

1 mi

Buckden

➡ At top end of car park go through gate with National Trust Upper Wharfedale sign beside it.

➡ Climb rough track for almost ¾ mile to hilltop.

① ➡ Soon after top of rise, bear **left** as track splits.

➡ Path becomes grassy after next gate. Keep **straight on** when you lose guiding wall on left.

➡ After third gate, watch for fingerpost on right.

② ➡ At fingerpost pass through gate on **left**.

➡ **Descend** stony path worn into bedrock and then continue beside wall for 140 yards to wall corner.

56 Short Walks Made Easy

☆ Election Bridge

The original bridge over the River Wharfe at Buckden was destroyed by a flood in 1748. The stone bridge that carries the road over the river today was built later in the 18th century. It is known as Election Bridge because its construction formed part of an electoral pledge made by a prospective MP.

✝ ■ JB Priestley

The Bradford-born dramatist JB Priestley, probably best known for his play *An Inspector Calls*, was a big fan of the Dales and Hubberholme in particular. Although he never lived in the parish, special permission was granted for his ashes to be buried at St Michael and All Angels Church in Hubberholme after he died in 1984 at the age of 89. The exact location of his ashes has never been revealed.

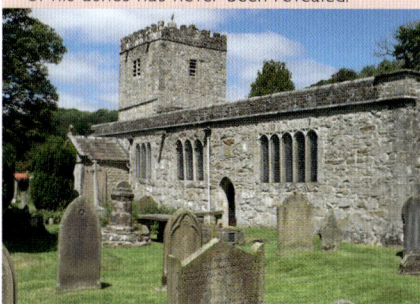

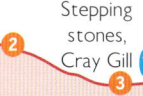

Stepping stones, Cray Gill ☕ The White Lion Inn

Cray

1½ miles

Cray Gill

3 ■ At corner, turn **right**; drop to gate in 50 yards.
■ Go through gate, cross Cray Gill (stepping stones when water is high). Cross road and take track opposite, behind pub.
■ This quickly forks. Bear **right** to next fork in 250 yards.

4 ■ Here, bear **left** (downhill).
■ Step across one track and immediately turn **right** along second track to reach cottage gateway.

Walk 7 Upper Wharfedale at Buckden 57

NATURE NOTES

As walkers ascend Buckden Rake at the start of the walk, there is a progression of plant species according to altitude. At first, there is a mix of woodland and open grassland. Here, you're likely to see hawthorn, elder, sycamore, ash, hazel, holly, forget-me-not, red clover, meadow buttercup, speedwell and lady's bedstraw. Higher, as the trees are left behind, you'll also see wild thyme, bird's-foot trefoil, biting stonecrop and common rock-rose. These last two both like well-drained soils, so are frequently seen in the limestone areas of the Yorkshire Dales, particularly surrounding rock outcrops.

Holly often forms part of the understorey in mature woodland. Its shiny leaves bring a splash of colour to the winter landscape when the surrounding trees have lost all their foliage.

Hawthorn can often be found growing on open hillsides and in hedgerows. Its highly scented, white flowers are often referred to as May blossom, named after the month in which they proliferate.

Although you're unlikely to see one, listen in springtime for the call of the cuckoo in Upper Wharfedale. These migratory birds don't spend long in the UK. They arrive in April and usually leave in June. There's no need for the adults to linger here – there are no young to feed and raise; they get other species to do that for them.

St Michael and All Angels; JB Priestley

 The George Inn

2 miles   2½ miles   Hubberholme

5 ▰ Just before it, bear **left** along trail, soon passing through wall. (Turning easy to miss in summer when grass is high.)
▰ After small gate, path heads **downhill** across hillside, then through beckside woods to reach wall stile.

6 ▰ After stile, meadow path is less clear. Keep close to riverbank for 250 yards.
▰ Cross wall stile and turn **right** along road.
▰ Cross River Wharfe at Hubberholme, turn **left** along lane and walk to field gate on left in ½ mile.

58   Short Walks Made Easy

Biting stonecrop

Above: forget-me-nots
Below: brown hare

Cuckoo

R i v e r W h a r f e

3 miles | 3½ miles | Election Bridge | Buckden

7 ➤ Go **left** through farm gate. Meadow track leads to riverside path.
➤ Having followed river for just over ½ mile, path swings away from water towards gate.

8 ➤ Go through gate. Turn **left** on road for 200 yards.
➤ On edge of Buckden, turn **left** along track beside village green.
➤ Cross B6160 diagonally **left** to follow access lane into car park.

Walk 7 Upper Wharfedale at Buckden **59**

Opposite (clockwise):
Black Bull Hotel,
Reeth; Station Inn,
Ribblehead
This page (clockwise):
The George &
Dragon, Dent; The
Lister Arms, Malham;
Yorkshire puddings;
The Bake-well Café,
Askrigg; The Sun Inn,
Dent

WALK 8

HORTON IN RIBBLESDALE

GO BY TRAIN

OS information
SD 803726 Explorer OL2
Distance 2.5 miles/4km
Time 1¼ hours
Start/Finish Horton in Ribblesdale Station
Parking BD24 0HL Station car park for rail users only; BD24 0HG National Park's Horton in Ribblesdale pay-and-display car park
Public toilets National Park car park
Cafés/pubs Horton in Ribblesdale
Terrain Pavement, rough lane and meadows. Exposed tree roots on riverside path
Hilliness Level, apart from station driveway
Footwear Winter 🥾 Spring/Summer/Autumn 👟

The lovely village of Horton in Ribblesdale lies on the banks of the River Ribble. Squeezed between two of Yorkshire's highest peaks – Ingleborough to the west and Pen-y-ghent to the east – it is a popular destination for hikers with their sights set on the hills. The valley itself also offers superb walking, through gorgeous meadows and along riverside paths with excellent views of the surrounding hills. Avoid the mad dash for a parking space by using the Settle–Carlisle Railway.

62 Short Walks Made Easy

Did you know? There are caves and potholes dotted about this area, including Gaping Gill, one of Britain's largest underground chambers. Here, a few miles west of Horton in Ribblesdale, Fell Beck plummets into a massive hole in the ground, falling more than 300 feet before it reaches the floor of the cavern.

Local legend The origins of the name Pen-y-ghent have been lost in the mists of time. 'Pen' is a Celtic word for 'top' as in 'summit', but the 'ghent' part is less certain. It could mean 'border' or, more likely, 'heathen', a word often used to describe the Norse people who settled in some upland regions of northern England.

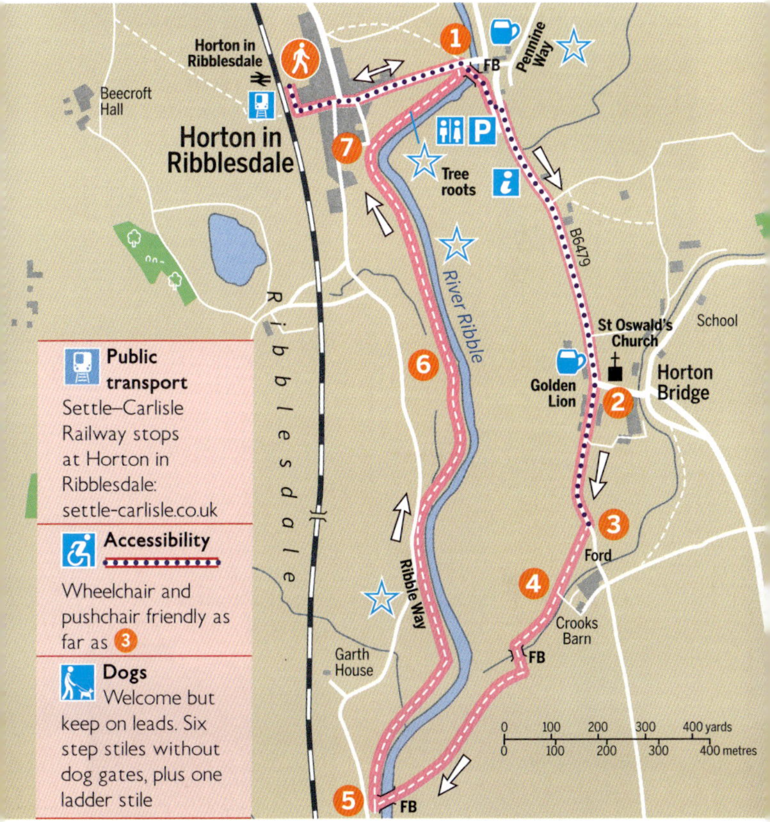

Public transport
Settle–Carlisle Railway stops at Horton in Ribblesdale: settle-carlisle.co.uk

Accessibility
Wheelchair and pushchair friendly as far as ③

Dogs Welcome but keep on leads. Six step stiles without dog gates, plus one ladder stile

Walk 8 Horton in Ribblesdale 63

STORIES BEHIND THE WALK

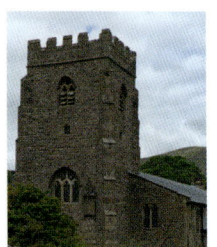

✝ **St Oswald's Church** The village church was built in the early part of the 12th century and still retains many of its Norman features, including an impressive nave. Other original features include the patterned moulding on the arch over the south door and a stone tub-font with herringbone decoration. The tower was added in the 14th century, with bells installed in the 17th century.

☆ **The Yorkshire Three Peaks** Horton in Ribblesdale is the traditional start and finish point for the Yorkshire Three Peaks, one of Britain's most famous challenge walks. It involves hikers climbing Ingleborough, Pen-y-ghent and Yorkshire's highest hill, Whernside, in less than 12 hours. The route is about 24 miles long with roughly 5,000 feet of ascent. It also forms the focus of an annual fell race, the record time for the current course being two hours and 46 minutes.

Horton in Ribblesdale Station

River Ribble

National Park car park

Pennine Way

1½ mile

①
- From station platform, walk into car park and head **downhill** on access lane.
- At the bottom, keep **straight ahead** at two road junctions and walk along pavement beside B6479 to road bridge.

①
- Just before road crosses River Ribble, bear **right** to use footbridge.
- Surfaced path leads into car park.
- Leave car park via vehicle access on **left** and turn **right** along B6479 to reach Golden Lion Hotel,

64 Short Walks Made Easy

☆ River Ribble

The River Ribble rises close to the Ribblehead Viaduct and flows sedately through Horton in Ribblesdale on its 75-mile journey to the Irish Sea. It also passes through Settle, Clitheroe, Ribchester and Preston. The latter served as a trading port from the 12th century until 1981 when regular dredging of the river made operations financially unviable.

☆ Pennine Way

The 268-mile Pennine Way passes through Horton in Ribblesdale on its way from Edale in Derbyshire to Kirk Yetholm in Scottish Borders. The idea for the long-distance walk was first mooted in 1935 by Tom Stephenson who started devising a route using existing paths. However, because 70 miles of new rights of way were also required, it wasn't until 1965 that Britain's first National Trail could be officially opened.

2
- Immediately after Golden Lion, take stony track off road on **right**.
- Follow it for 300 yards to signposted stile.

3
- Climb stile in wall on **right**.
- Cross small field diagonally **left** to use ladder stile on far side.
- Continue in same direction through grass for 25 yards to rejoin track. Turn **right**.

Walk 8 Horton in Ribblesdale 65

NATURE NOTES

Top: lady's bedstraw
Above: meadow buttercup

There's an interesting variety of habitats on this walk. Like so many of the hay meadows encountered in the Yorkshire Dales, the grassland between ③ and ⑤ is brought to colourful life in spring and summer. Species include pignut, red clover and, creating a vast carpet of yellow in the large meadow nearest the River Ribble, meadow buttercup.

As well as being lightly wooded in places, the riverbank plays host to yet more wildflowers, including lady's bedstraw. Soft, springy and with a pleasant, hay-like smell, this was once used to fill mattresses. Butterbur can be seen on the damp ground approaching ⑦. Its heart-shaped leaves can grow to three feet in diameter on stalks as tall as five feet.

We don't often get a chance to see the underground network formed by tree roots but watch for sycamore trees after ⑦ to see where the river has washed away the soil, exposing the entanglement below. The banks along this part of the river are also home to several beech trees, the leaves of which turn a coppery orange in the autumn.

River Ribble

⑤

1½ miles
Ribble Way

④ ▸ When track bends left after 120 yards, take waymarked trail through grass on **right**.
▸ Cross footbridge and turn **right** on grassy meadow path, reaching wooden bridge over River Ribble in 400 yards.

⑤ ▸ Having crossed, turn **right** along riverside trail – signposted Ribble Way, Horton.
▸ Path crosses several stiles and tributary bridges: it's clear on ground for more than ½ mile to third stile.

Short Walks Made Easy

Top right: beech leaves in autumn
Top left: tree roots
Left: butterbur

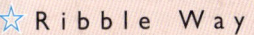

☆ Ribble Way

6 ■ Path less clear beyond gated stile. Simply keep to riverbank for next 200 yards.
■ Route more obvious again after next stile; **continue** for 250 yards to gate in wall.

7 ■ Use gate in wall on **right**, ignoring grassy track ahead.
■ Walk along riverbank for 250 yards.
■ **Climb** railed steps in wall to rejoin outward route at **1**, turning **left** to return to station.

Walk 8 Horton in Ribblesdale 67

WALK 9

RIVER WHARFE AT GRASSINGTON

The attractive market town of Grassington sits close to the banks of the River Wharfe in the south-east corner of the Yorkshire Dales National Park. A short stroll from the town leads down to Linton Falls, where the river negotiates the narrowing channel. With the Wharfe proving a spirited companion, our walk then heads upstream along its wildflower-lined banks. The final part of the route passes through meadows and along lanes before walkers are lured by the plethora of cafés and pubs surrounding Grassington's market square.

OS information
SE 002637
Explorer OL2

Distance
2 miles/3.2km

Time
1 hour

Start/Finish
Grassington

Parking BD23 5AP
National Park's Grassington pay-and-display car park

Public toilets
In car park

Cafés/pubs
Grassington

Terrain
Surfaced paths and pavements in town; riverside trail and meadows; quiet road

Hilliness
Moderate descent to river at start; steady ascent from river near end

Footwear
Winter
Spring/Summer/Autumn

Public transport
DalesBus services 72/72A/72B, 74/74A, 822 and 874/875: dalesbus.org

Accessibility
Road sections wheelchair friendly; suitable for all-terrain pushchairs throughout

Dogs
Welcome but keep on leads. No stiles

Did you know? Every year, usually in September, thousands of people, many in military uniforms and retro dresses, descend on Grassington for its 1940s Weekend. Vintage vehicles can be seen around the market square while the music of the decade can be heard coming from the pubs and shops. And, for those who know how to swing, big bands take to the Town Hall stage to provide evening entertainment.

Local legend Grassington was the scene of a notorious murder in the 18th century when local man Tom Lee killed the town's doctor. At first, Lee thought he'd got away with the crime after a lack of evidence caused the case against him to collapse, but he was eventually found guilty at York in 1768. He was later hanged.

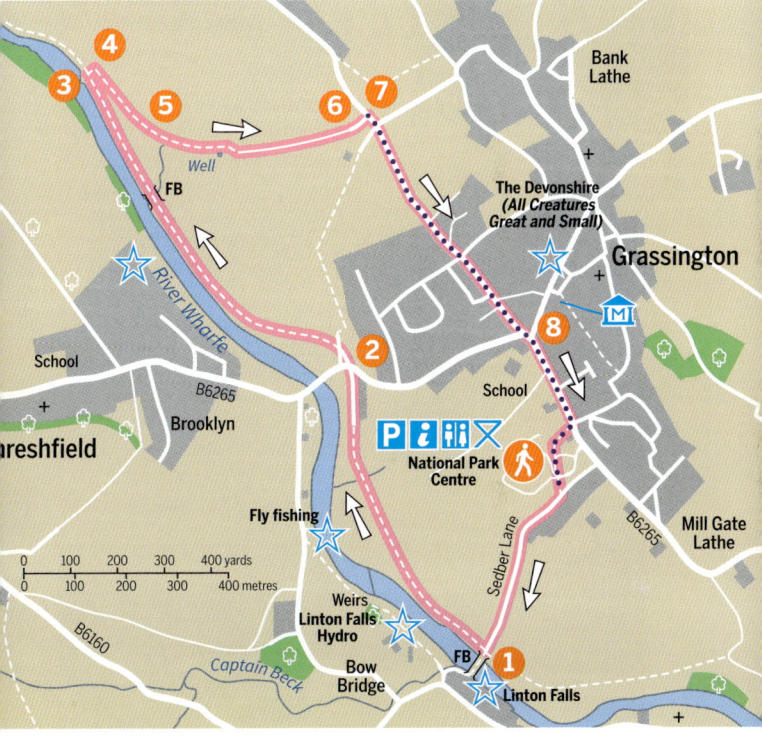

Walk 9 River Wharfe at Grassington

STORIES BEHIND THE WALK

☆ **Fly fishing** The River Wharfe is regarded by many as one of the best fly-fishing destinations in Yorkshire. It contains good stocks of wild brown trout. Grayling can be found in the river too. The Yorkshire Dales Rivers Trust has carried out a lot of work on pollution control along the length of the river. It has also fenced off long stretches of riverbank to restrict grazing, thereby allowing vegetation to thrive and preventing excess sediment from entering the water.

☆ **Linton Falls** Above the footbridge near ①, the River Wharfe is a relatively placid affair. When it reaches the bridge though, a geological fault causes it to drop several feet. Forced into a narrowing limestone channel here, it suddenly takes on a more ferocious nature that is best seen (and heard!) after heavy rain.

National Park car park

Sedber Lane

Linton Falls ☆ ①

☆ Linton Falls Hydro ½ mile

☆ River Wharfe

- Facing away from road, walk to bottom left-hand corner of car park and through small gate in wall.
- Turn **right** along walled path (Sedber Lane) to reach River Wharfe.

① - To see Linton Falls, **cross** footbridge and head **left** to viewing area.
- **Re-cross** bridge to use small gate on **left**.
- After 200 yards, route and river briefly separate. Keep **straight ahead** on grassy path to road.

70 Short Walks Made Easy

☆ **Linton Falls Hydro** The River Wharfe at Grassington was first used to generate electricity for local homes and businesses in 1909, but the plant, located on the upper Linton weir, ceased operations in 1948 when the National Grid was nationalised. The tiny power station was reopened in 2012 at a cost of £500,000 and is now able to generate enough power to meet the average energy needs of 90 homes.

☆ *All Creatures Great and Small* Like Askrigg, Grassington has been used in the filming of *All Creatures Great and Small*. But while Askrigg was used in the original TV series, Grassington plays the role of the fictional Darrowby in the new version, first televised in 2020. The Devonshire pub, like the Kings Arms in Askrigg, becomes the all-important village pub, the fictional Drovers Arms. Grassington also featured in the 1992 film *Wuthering Heights* staring Juliette Binoche and Ralph Fiennes.

☆ Fly fishing

☆ River Wharfe

1 mile

2 ➧ Carefully **cross** B6265 and take broad, stony path into trees opposite.
➧ After just 35 yards, go **over** rough track and through gate.
➧ Path returns to riverbank. Walk with river on left.

3 ➧ About 300 yards after crossing tributary stream bridge, go through small gate in fence on **right**, beside fingerpost.

Walk 9 River Wharfe at Grassington

NATURE NOTES

The River Wharfe and its banks are home to a wide range of wildlife. While brown trout and smaller fish inhabit the water itself, mallard, black-headed gull, grey wagtail, heron, goosander and dipper can be seen on the surface. If you're lucky, you might catch sight of the blue flash of a kingfisher.

Among the species that thrive on the banks are meadow cranesbill, meadow buttercup, thistle, ragwort, red clover, common rock-rose, lady's bedstraw, butterbur and trees such as hawthorn, ash and sycamore. Some members of the pea family can also be seen, including meadow vetchling, which climbs around other plants for support, and cow vetch, a pretty, purple flower that is also known as 'tufted vetch' or 'bird vetch'. Watch too for the pink, pea-like flowers of common restharrow, often found in limestone areas such as the Dales. This plant has particularly tough roots and gets its name from the fact that it could stop a horse-drawn harrow in its tracks.

Above: cow vetch
Opposite: **top**, common restharrow; **middle**, meadow vetchling; **bottom**, dipper

1½ miles

4 ➡ Path isn't obvious now. Turning sharp **right**, initially aim to left of row of houses in distance.
➡ Reach fingerpost at wall corner in 90 yards. Walk with wall on left to wall/fence corner.

5 ➡ At corner, go through gate on **left**. Swing **half-right** on grassy path, passing 15 yards to left of power pole.
➡ Beyond next gate, grassy path swings up to **left** for 250 yards to reach set of gates.

72 Short Walks Made Easy

Kingfisher

Village Centre *All Creatures Great and Small* National Park car park
(200 yards)

2 miles

6 ➡ Pass through gates (about 50 yards to left of detached house).
➡ Follow stony track for 35 yards to surfaced lane.

7 ➡ Turn **right** and walk along the lane for 550 yards to junction in Grassington. (There is no pavement, but traffic is generally light.)

8 ➡ Turn **left** at T-junction. To visit village centre, immediately turn **left** again – up Main Street.
➡ Otherwise, follow main road round to **right** for 180 yards to use zebra crossing and re-enter car park.

Walk 9 River Wharfe at Grassington

WALK 10

MALHAM COVE

Malham Cove is one of the most spectacular natural features in the Yorkshire Dales, if not the whole of England. This massive, 260-foot-high limestone cliff forms a majestic, curving amphitheatre that towers over beautiful, wildflower-filled meadows. A popular, well-constructed path leads walkers to the base of the dazzling white cliff. While less mobile visitors will then return the way they came, others can cross the beck that springs from the base of the rock wall and follow less well-used meadow paths back to the village.

OS information

SD 899627
Explorer OL2

Distance
2.1 miles/3.4km

Time
1¼ hours

Start/Finish
Malham

Parking BD23 4DJ
Malham's National Park car park

Public toilets
In car park

Cafés/pubs
Malham village

Terrain
Stony tracks, quiet road, surfaced path and meadow paths. When wet, exposed limestone on short ascent between ④ and ⑤ is slippery

Hilliness
Gently undulating, with one short, steeper climb between ④ and ⑤

Footwear
Winter 🥾
Spring/Summer/Autumn 👟

74 Short Walks Made Easy

Did you know? Malham Cove is a favourite location among film makers. In *Harry Potter and the Deathly Hallows part 1*, filmed in 2009, the cove is one of the places visited by Harry and Hermione. The expanse of strange-looking limestone pavement at the top of the cliff was the shooting location for a scene in Peter Kosminsky's 1992 film *Emily Brontë's Wuthering Heights*.

Public transport
DalesBus services 75, 201/211, 881 and 884: dalesbus.org

Accessibility
Wheelchair and pushchair friendly from 1 to 4, with return to start via outward route

Dogs
Welcome but keep on leads. No stiles

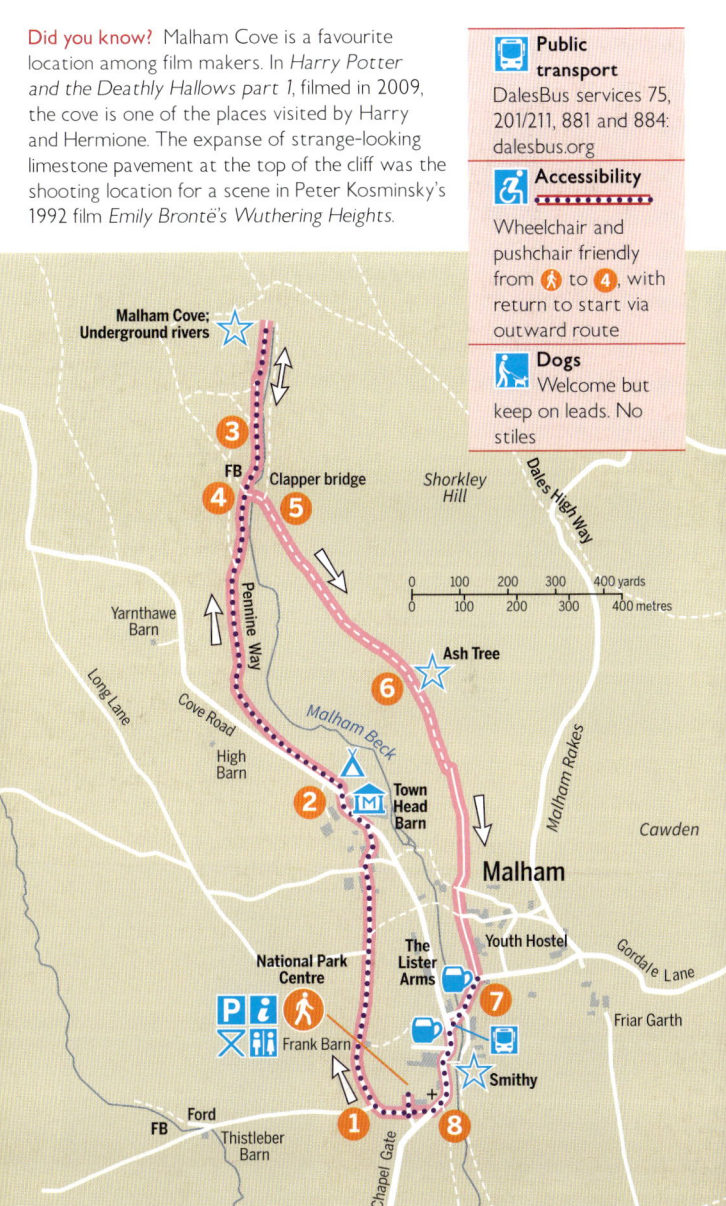

Walk 10 Malham Cove 75

STORIES BEHIND THE WALK

 Town Head Barn This is the chance for passing visitors to see the interior of a traditional Yorkshire Dales barn. Town Head Barn also houses an exhibition on local farming practices. Opened to the public in 1997, the barn forms part of a massive National Trust estate that includes Malham Tarn, nearly three miles to the north. The conservation charity's interest in the area began in 1946 when the tarn and surrounding land were gifted to it.

☆ Underground rivers

Like Winterscales Beck at Ribblehead (see Walk 6), Malham Beck flows underground for part of its course. Rising on Malham Moor, it disappears into the permeable limestone and then emerges again at the foot of the cliff at Malham Cove. It was once thought that Malham Beck originated in Malham Tarn, but experiments using dyes have shown the two streams take different routes underground.

Town Head Barn

Campsite entrance

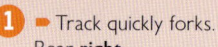

National Park car park

1
- Walk to car park's vehicle entrance and, drawing level with large, wooden Yorkshire Dales sign on left, take rough track on **right**.

1
- Track quickly forks. Bear **right**.
- Turn **right** at next track junction.
- On reaching road, turn **left**. Walk on asphalt for 100 yards to campsite entrance.

76 Short Walks Made Easy

☆ Malham Cove

The Malham Cove crag was formed at the end of the last glacial period when meltwater from a retreating glacier poured over the Mid Craven Fault, a massive rock fracture that had been caused by earlier movements beneath the Earth's crust. The cliff top is home to one of most substantial areas of limestone pavement in Great Britain. Here, because of the susceptibility of the rock to weathering and erosion, limestone blocks (or clints) have formed divided by fissures known as grykes.

☆ Smithy

The old smithy in the village used to be owned by blacksmith and artist Bill Wild, who worked here from 1946 until his death in 1985. He bequeathed it to the local church, and it is now let to Annabelle Bradley, who continues the traditional skills by creating both artistic and functional wrought ironwork. She also runs metal-working courses and opens a small viewing area for visitors.

1 mile

Clapper bridge over Malham Beck

2 ▸ Here, go through pedestrian gate in wall on **right**. Follow surfaced path.
▸ About ⅓ mile beyond campsite, see clapper bridge on right **4**. Ignore for now, but route returns to this point.
▸ **Continue** to next gate.

3 ▸ Soon after gate, bear **right** at fork in path, staying close to beck. Follow path until it ends near cliff wall.
▸ Return to clapper bridge.

Walk 10 Malham Cove 77

NATURE NOTES

In spring and summer, the meadows and verges around Malham are characterised by the wildflowers that will now be familiar to readers. These include biting stonecrop, meadow cranesbill, oxeye daisy, meadow buttercup, bird's-foot trefoil and yellow loosestrife. On exposed limestone, including at the base of the crag, watch for wild thyme and the tentacle-like fronds of maidenhair spleenwort.

Herons, often as still as statues, can be seen fishing in Malham Beck all year round, while a much swifter bird nests on the nearby cliff ledges... Peregrine falcons, the fastest animals on the planet, have been successfully rearing young here since 1993.

On the return to Malham, soon after ⑥, watch for a massive ash tree to the left of the path. The ash dieback fungus has affected thousands of trees across England since it was first seen in this country in 2012, but, for the time being, this specimen appears to be healthy.

Ash tree

Malham Cove; Underground river

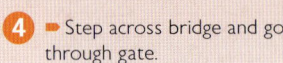
Clapper bridge over Malham Beck

1½ miles

④ ▪ Step across bridge and go through gate.
▪ Route unclear on ground now. Faint trail rises diagonally **right** across rough slope ahead.

⑤ ▪ At top of slope, faint trail passes to **right** of walls (small, ruined building). Continue with field wall on left to pass through gap in 100 yards.
▪ Go **straight over** next field and through gate.

78 Short Walks Made Easy

Top left: heron
Top right: yellow loosestrife
Above: Maidenhair spleenwort
Left: wild thyme

6 ➥ More definite, mostly fenced path leads through meadows for ⅓ mile.
➥ Keep **ahead** on joining surfaced lane near cottages to reach The Lister Arms.

7 ➥ At T-junction, turn **right** along road, soon crossing humpback bridge over Malham Beck.
➥ Go **left** at next junction. Walk along road for 200 yards to Methodist chapel.

8 ➥ Turn **right** after chapel and **right** again after National Park Centre to re-enter car park.

2 miles

Walk 10 Malham Cove 79

Publishing information

© Crown copyright 2023.
All rights reserved.

Ordnance Survey, OS, and the OS logos are registered trademarks, and OS Short Walks Made Easy is a trademark of Ordnance Survey Ltd.

© Crown copyright and database rights (2023) Ordnance Survey.

ISBN 978 0 319092 59 0
1st edition published by Ordnance Survey 2023.

www.ordnancesurvey.co.uk

While every care has been taken to ensure the accuracy of the route directions, the publishers cannot accept responsibility for errors or omissions, or for changes in details given. The countryside is not static: hedges and fences can be removed, stiles can be replaced by gates, field boundaries can alter, footpaths can be rerouted and changes in ownership can result in the closure or diversion of some concessionary paths. Also, paths that are easy and pleasant for walking in fine conditions may become slippery, muddy and difficult in wet weather.

If you find an inaccuracy in either the text or maps, please contact Ordnance Survey at os.uk/contact.

All rights reserved. No part of this publication may be reproduced, transmitted in any form or by any means, or stored in a retrieval system without either the prior written permission of the publisher, or in the case of reprographic reproduction a licence issued in accordance with the terms and licences issued by the CLA Ltd.

A catalogue record for this book is available from the British Library.

Milestone Publishing credits

Author: Vivienne Crow

Series editor: Kevin Freeborn

Maps: Cosmographics

Design and Production: Patrick Dawson, Milestone Publishing

Printed in India by Replika Press Pvt. Ltd

Photography credits

Front cover: Alex Manders/Shutterstock.com. **Back cover** cornfield/Shutterstock.com.

All photographs supplied by the author ©Vivienne Crow except page 6 Debbie North.

The following images were supplied by Shutterstock.com: pages 1 high fliers; 19 seawhisper; 33 Stephan Morris; 39 Werner Baumgarten; 40 davidrobertsphotography; 41 Anne Coatesy; 41 Sandra Standbridge; 41 Andrew Fletcher; 59 godi photo; 59 Simon C Stobart; 59 Sanuta; 60 DronG; 63 mountaintreks; 73 Rudmer Zwerver.